POETIC THOUGHTS, EXPRESSIONS AND CONVICTIONS

POETIC THOUGHTS, EXPRESSIONS AND CONVICTIONS

J.L. PRICE

Poetic Thoughts, Expressions and Convictions

Copyright © 2022 by J.L. Price. All rights reserved.

No part of this publication may be reproduced, stored in a retrieval system or transmitted in any way by any means, electronic, mechanical, photocopy, recording or otherwise without the prior permission of the author except as provided by USA copyright law.

The opinions expressed by the author are not necessarily those of URLink Print and Media.

1603 Capitol Ave., Suite 310 Cheyenne, Wyoming USA 82001
1-888-980-6523 | admin@urlinkpublishing.com

URLink Print and Media is committed to excellence in the publishing industry.

Book design copyright © 2022 by URLink Print and Media. All rights reserved.

Published in the United States of America

Library of Congress Control Number: 2022912598
ISBN 978-1-68486-224-5 (Paperback)
ISBN 978-1-68486-225-2 (Digital)

24.06.22

CONTENTS

Introduction 9
One Letter, one word one poem 11
Something to offer you 12
Just one Poem 13
It's a new season 14
If I had a hammer 15
A day for myself 16
An ode to poetry 17
When you find the missing piece 19
Living in a world without music 20
Grinding 21
Let Freedom and justice ring! 22
Blow your horn 23
Go to work! 24
In my mind and in my heart 25
You can't teach an old dog a new trick 26
Fun with Haikus 27
The absence of a smile 29
Rainbow Seeker 31
In your season 32
Spring's Arrival 33
Short poems 34
A black and white dream 35
Flip side to Love's Glory 36
Before you say yes 37
The Journey Begins 38
The power of a smile 39
Your spoken words 40
Make it Happen! 41
When you are who you are 42
Dark days 44

Squirrels in the attic	45
Sunshine	46
Laments of a fan	47
When it rains	49
Preaching to the choir	50
Inside the spiral notebook	52
Hide me from the rain	53
A piece of heaven?	54
I receive it!	55
He sustains me	56
Ready for a change	58
I am ready for change	59
Music: The Queen of my Soul	60
All Aboard! Riding with Harriet Tubman	62
All aboard! All aboard! Destination: Freedom!	63
We Lived with a Legend Maya Angelou	65
Introduction: The Black Soldier	66
A tribute to the Black Soldier	67
They were Buffalo Soldiers	68
Ready & Forward the motto of the 10th cavalry	70
Oh what a day!	72
Out of the Darkness	73
Save the children	75
How deep is my love	76
24-7 and 365 A love that won't go away	77
Insurgency in America	78
The Cost of a Smile	79
Let your voice be heard	80
Gold	81
Alone	82
I look to the hills Psalm 121	83
This is not America	85
Finding peace through the storm	86
Speaking his own thoughts	87
If I Could (A tribute to women of color)	88
Inhale Exhale Just breathe	90

Look on the bright side 92
Accountability 94
Don't Worry be happy 96
Soul Searching 98
Reflections 99
Epilog 101

INTRODUCTION

Greetings! I have written three books in my lifetime. My first book was a devotional. I later penned two books of poetry. Inside writing poetry I found myself and my calling. I never sold a large number of books, but I experienced so much personal joy from writing them. As I reflect, I am hopefully that my work has touched someone in their struggles or if nothing else it made someone feel good. Even if it was just for a few moments.

    This offering is special to me because I was able to touch on so many situations going on in the world today. Our world is so full on discontent and grouping of people. Social injustices, Black Lives Matter and women's rights highlight almost every newscast. The state of America is very fragile as we attempt to recover from a worldwide Pandemic which has impacted everyone and taken thousands of lives.

    Through it all life goes on and we each have to hold dear to the things that make us who we are. We also should dare ourselves to try something new because inside of those thoughts none of us know how much time we will be here. Do everything that you can to enjoy yourselves. May each reader find joy if only for just a moment inside this book of poetic thoughts.

J. L. Price

ONE LETTER, ONE WORD ONE POEM

This whole thing starts off with one word which will be the first of more than 14,000. Inside those words, I hope you will be able to see what type of person that I really am. I always try to write with conviction and most of all truth. I don't have a solution to many of the problems of the world today, but I do have thoughts, expressions and convictions on how we can deal with some of them. Read them all as you go through each poem or each section. This was a labor of love.

SOMETHING TO OFFER YOU

Stretch out your hands all across this land
This world is calling for a common connection
its time to unite and offer love to those that are displaced
and to the many who have lost their smile.
Now is the time to live in the truth and manufacture
the power to make our world and our lives better.

That something that I offer you is poetry.
I trust that its message will refresh your soul and give you
empowerment to even make you bold!

I offer you my poetry.

JUST ONE POEM

I want my words to be refreshing like cold spring water from a sparkling natural spring. I want my poetry to comfort and soothe like an afternoon breeze and catapult you into relaxation or at other times— action. I want it to help you to recover that smile and chuckle that now seems to constantly go away. I want you to live it and to enjoy it right now on this day! Let it re-affirm to you that others have the same tribulations!

May this work take you down memory lane and have you yearn for how things once were and how they used to be. I say without hesitation this is what I want you to see. Well, if it does then I have succeeded in my purpose! May a poem— just one written poem maybe become a favorite of yours. Maybe you will offer it to a friend in need. Maybe it will help you to plant a seed. I hope this and more is here for you in just one little poem.

IT'S A NEW SEASON

Let this new season be not just for the beginning of a New Year
let it be a season for change for you and me
let it be a change for the better
a time to move in a new direction or seek a new destiny
this new season can allow you to let go of the past
and even rid yourself of relationships that did not last
A new season to remove stumbling blocks
move them to the side and clear your way
New connections will have to be made and new goals
must be set
let it be a season for change— your change and mine

IF I HAD A HAMMER

If I had a hammer
I would knock out world poverty—followed by deceit and then use my hammer to create sincerity and trust between people of all colors.

If I had a hammer
I would hammer out police brutality—I'd hammer out infidelity and make relationships between men and women again strong!

I'd hammer out human idols present on social media who are supported in the form of thousands upon thousands of followers. Collusion and a government that caters to the one percent would also fill the wrath of my hammer.

If I had a hammer—I would hammer into everyone a desire to excel and be the best they can be.

All by myself, I cannot change the world, but I can change myself. The best part is I do not need a hammer to do it. Oh, by the way, neither do you!

A DAY FOR MYSELF

Hello world!
I am going to take a day for myself
I'm not being mean
Today I won't worry about anyone else
I will relax
Release tension
and say no to dissension!
Only positive thought will I mention
Maybe I will sleep late
All appointments can just wait
No TV shows will I hate!
I'll just close my eyes
I'll feel myself fly
Gently, I will touch down
Preferably with no one around!
Remember: This is a day for myself
I won't take any calls
This is my choice
It comes at a moment's notice
I don't want to hear anyone's voice!
Just peace and quiet
I'm going to do it- I am not asking anyone to buy it
And If I chose-I will even get off my diet!
No loud music
just peace and calm
No situations to cause any harm
No situations where I have to flex
And in a moment's notice wonder what will come next
Because this is the day I've deemed just for myself
And when it is over again I will then worry about everyone else!

AN ODE TO POETRY

I have written so much about you over the past years. As a matter of fact, I have fallen in love with you over and over again! I own a pen that will never run dry, so I always will have something good to say and write about you. I have shared encouraging laughs with you. You make me feel good about myself.

Through the ink of my pen, you've been there to see and even felt my silent and my visible tears. I am not ashamed for you to see me cry. You have been like a well that never go dry. I can always count on you for a drink of encouragement. When I was so low and could not see above the curb, you gave me the incentive to get up and be an encouragement to someone else!

You encouraged me to not waste time wallowing in sorrow. To take up my pen and be a blessing to someone. With you in my life I can do what I am called to do and that my friend is write and recite poetry. So I salute you again. You will always have a special place in my heart.

Thought for the day #1

Truth and devotion

Live each new day with truth and devotion do not be overcome by the world. Keep your plans in motion.

WHEN YOU FIND THE MISSING PIECE

Life is somewhat like a jigsaw puzzle. We spend many years trying to find the right piece to make our lives complete. As we all know that for many of us; it is not an easy feat. During our lifetime so many of us sadly will never find that missing piece! When we find that right piece; it all seems to come together and at that moment its complete.

There is no more forcing! It's kind of like trying to fit a square piece into an oblong section. When it fits both parties involved truly know! No one after seeing how they have meshed together should ever try to separate what is now a complete picture! Through all of life's ups and downs and its many highs and lows, good and bad relationships don't ever stop looking for your missing piece!

LIVING IN A WORLD WITHOUT MUSIC

What would life be like without music? Periods of silence—no songs. All talk radio no music stations to calm, motivate or inspire the nations. There would be no vocalists to sing songs of love or even the blues. Many people like myself would be lost without a clue. All commercials would be minus that musical jingle no verses so strong they make your insides tingle.

There would be quiet journeys on trips by plane, bus, or car only folks sitting and chatting at restaurants or bars. There wouldn't be any music cds, music sites or apps to give us that private or personal feeling. These things we all take for granted so many of us would be reeling! There would be no nursery rhymes, national anthems, or college fight songs.

We would be begging for answers— just what went wrong? No classical, soul, hip hop or gospel would forever again grace our ears. There would be no songs to announce the coming of the bride. How dull would that be our emotions we can't hide! We would be void of sheet music, teachers, or instructors to rely on all this would let us know that the world suddenly doesn't have a song!

There would be no toy instruments to mold kids into music and if music wasn't around tell me how did we ever do it? So, for me music is the queen of my soul I will enjoy it forever and even more as I grow old! What would my world be like without music? I don't want to know!

GRINDING

All my life I have been exploring and climbing and trying to find just who I am. Though when I look back at my life, I did not take enough chances. I did not allow myself enough dances with destiny or the things that could have been. I was not encouraged to step out on faith and for goals I wanted to achieve I simply put them away. In my mind I said they would be accomplished on another day. Yet father time cannot be put on hold. The clock just keeps right on ticking. Each day that we awake offers an opportunity to carve out your own space. Its an opportunity to take your place and to start to work to get where you want to be. So, to you I say envision yourself shining just as the star that you are. Keep on defining the good qualities that people see when they talk or come into contact with you. Keep rising, ascending and make your goals unending. To keep it short—just keep grinding.

LET FREEDOM AND JUSTICE RING!

You stood for us visually as our own black king
In the course of your work you helped freedom to ring
your actions push black voices to sing
heightening our awareness about so many things

Not taking no for an answer— you wanted more
You knocked hard very hard on those closed doors!
Those actions would force society to change
letting them know that you weren't playing games

Freedom, more jobs and equality— give us respect!
Many years later; America is still not there yet
but because of your mission you weren't afraid,
so we still must follow the path you helped lay

You led with power, authority, elegance and grace
you put so much pride on black America's face
through all of the mistreatment that you received
on top of that— of your life you were relieved

Though many years have passed since your tragic death
Over all black Americans have improved their self-worth
So let us continue to take pride in just who we are
Keep moving forward then brightly shine your own star

Never ever forget the work of Dr. Martin Luther King
To all of America Let freedom and justice ring!
Freedom, Equality and justice for all
Let it ring! Let it ring! Let it ring!

BLOW YOUR HORN

Blow your own horn
make your own sound
Blow your own horn
make it your new norm

Blow your own horn and blow it very loud
but not by being self-centered, arrogant, or hearing and not listening
Blow your own horn
because there is only one you.
You worked hard to be the best.
You are navigating through life and dealing with so many tests.
Blow your own horn.
learn the songs of life everyday— and as you blow help someone along the way.

Do not get caught up trying to be like someone else
follow your own road even as you encounter potholes and even dead-end streets.
Turn around and redirect, with determination in your mind there will be no defeat.

Blow your own horn
so melodic and with a distinct flavor that you grew and perfected.
Inspire someone to do their own thing.
And when you do it's their life you just affected.

GO TO WORK!

Believe you can accomplish anything your heart desires. You must set forth a plan to make it happen. Do not let anyone or anything stand in your way. You have to put the nay-sayers and the non-believers in their place. The roadblocks and the mountains have to be moved! Get up, get busy and know for yourself that you are a winner! Its time to go to work!

Former president the enigmatic Donald Trump took the office at the age of seventy. President Elect Joe Biden followed him as president at the seasoned age of seventy-seven. Stop telling yourself you are too old. It is never too late to change your fate. It is never too late to change your point of view. It's never too late to try something new.

The conditions of the world have many of us at home even more than we desire. Take advantage if you can; learn ways to take your aspirations higher. We can learn a new language, work hard to get physically in shape, learn how to paint or keep memoirs of your journey through this unforgiving time in our lives.

The list can go on and on— take a writing course, create a home project, and see it through to fruition, learn how to play a musical instrument or a different language. Whatever you do: It's time to go to work!

IN MY MIND AND IN MY HEART

At a moment's notice anyone can be taken away
So we should remember no one is here to forever stay!
For that reason, live life with little or few regrets
Make sure that you take on the challenge of what comes next

When loved ones are called home, carry a piece of them every day
the positive things they showed us will help us on our way
for life itself is just a part of the journey to be with our lord
May we all take solace in knowing that is a just reward

Forever and ever let them live in our mind and in our hearts

YOU CAN'T TEACH AN OLD DOG A NEW TRICK

America is institutionalized, glamorized, and viewed all over the world as the place to be. Let it be known there is no perfect place; yet America give you a chance to bake your own pie and even own the business! We can try but the American judicial system will never change! The system says justice for all but in most instance today we see little or no justice at all! We hype the black lives matter theme but make no efforts to change systematic racism and police brutality. America would rather pay lawsuits than to admit there's an issue with how people of color are treated.

Our sports stars take to the streets hoping to defeat but just like the old dog you attempt to teach; the old guard in America looks at you like you are crazy! They will let you holler, scream, rant, and rave just as long as you want but the old dog named America will never cave. He will never cave in! Sadly, America is embedded in its own ways. The only way there will be a change would be through the old dogs dying away and the voice of the millennials standing tall and stating it's a new day. Oh, how I wish this would happen!

FUN WITH HAIKUS

Haikus are short three-line poems that uses sensory language to capture a feeling or image. Haiku poetry were originally developed by Japanese poets. They are often inspired by nature, beauty, love or a heartfelt experience. There are many ways they can be presented even with humor. I hope that you will enjoy and appreciate the thought and simplicity of my style of haiku poetry.

Influence

When stroking a pen
One can influence many
Never forget that

It's gone!

A tiny snowflake
that falls from the sky it melts
before your eyes

Darkness to Light

You invaded my space
then you awakened my sleep
I'll call you sunlight

Covid dreams

I awake from dreams
hoping that covid is done
but it lingers on

Holding on

The stress of the world
Has everyone holding on to
hope of a new day

The River

Its destined by God
following his guided course
makes it to the sea

My Home

Inside you feel love
see hard work and gratitude
I welcome my guests

The Gift

Waking up this morn
with gratitude and thanksgiving
cherish each new day

THE ABSENCE OF A SMILE

I wish the world could smile more—like before. A smile can imply a sedate mind. It can show a freedom or confidence and a desire to do what one wants. Now more than ever our world and attitude are controlled by the media. Gloom and doom dominates the news. News flash: Please watch at your own risk! Rarely seldom will events of the world generate a smile or a happy thought for viewers. The world needs to smile again!

Its ok to watch the news from time to time but do not allow it to control your own personal thoughts! One must find things that make you smile and feel good about yourself and your own life. The world is what it is but that beautiful smile and your demeanor belongs to you!

Thought for the day #2

Dreams can come true

The best part of having a good dream is seeing it come true!

RAINBOW SEEKER

It's been about five years since I've seen your face
I can't believe you just appeared in this place!
You are a spirit lifter and a special sight to behold
after a September rain you quickly did unfold

Look, there is a rainbow
you just blessed me with your presence
As a rainbow seeker did I just win?
I don't know how long you will be here
so let the viewing began!

The uniqueness and beauty of your presence is
that you do not appear in multiple sightings.
It is part of your allure that's so captivating yet inviting.
Sunshine after the rain is fine but give me a rainbow anytime!

I got to take some pictures— to capture this moment
Click again and again I got great pics; I will call it success
I will view these again and again until I see my next
Old tales say there is a pot of gold at the rainbow's end
If that's true then let me take the first step over the rainbow
just as Dorothy and later Patti sang
Let me began my journey now and see what it will bring

You see I am a rainbow seeker
In the presence of a rainbow I feel a natural high
my issues are put on hold as I look into the sky
I close with my these thoughts:
"My spirits are lifted when I experience seeing a rainbow."
"A rainbow a day would take my gloom away."

IN YOUR SEASON

Don't take time and youthfulness for granted
time passes— we all get older!
So, in our season, we must be decisive
do not postpone things we can do today!
By making plans with short deadlines,
it ensures that our plans stay fresh on our mind

Keep in mind our season does not last for a lifetime
so we must attack our goals and desires with vigor
and tackle them with decisiveness!
So when we do –we can smile
with a sense of accomplishment for each battle fought
smile a little more with each battle won
because every day and every event will not always be fun!

All things in their own time!

SPRING'S ARRIVAL

At the cusp of the winter season my mind fast forwards to the arrival of spring. I say good-bye to those cold grey skies and hello to a bright golden sun. I anxiously await those colorful spring flowers; temper myself for some evening showers. I delight to the idea of once again planting my own garden. Though the work and upkeep are challenging but the rewards of my own homegrown vegetables far out way the time spent.

Then there are those peaceful walks exercise required! Manicuring the lawn and seeing the dew glistening in the morn. Yeah, I like that! Now the days are longer as I enjoy daylight savings time, sip on a cold glass of iced tea. These are some of the things that are waiting for me. An evening relaxing on the deck, with lots of time to reflect. I can now plan a trip without the threat of snow. I'm getting my bags packed so I am ready to go!

Finally I will simply sit and listen to Summer Breeze soulfully sang by the Isleys, or Summertime crooned by Fantasia. Either way, I cannot lose! The cold days of winter I will quickly forget. I will just continue my focus on what will come next. Springtime! Why did you take so long?

SHORT POEMS

These short poems are thought provoking. They were written to drive their point across quickly.

Are you sure?

Things we think are off
Many times they are still on
Things we think are broken
They sometimes remain strong!

A BLACK AND WHITE DREAM

As I descended the stairs,
I misjudged my step
down I tumbled
losing my breath
the scary part about it is
I was the only one around
in what seemed like split
seconds I was on the ground
then I awaken; so glad it was a dream--
so scary how so amazingly real it
seemed!

FLIP SIDE TO LOVE'S GLORY

The story of love we know does not always tell of success
Many of our relationships can sour and then digress
Many to the extent that it should be severed and ended
All things aren't meant to be, and some things can't be mended

BEFORE YOU SAY YES

Before you say yes,
Is that answer in your best— interest that is?
Many will request a quick answer and give you little choice
But please, please remember that you too have a voice
So take time to consider the lasting effects of saying the word yes
And what you might find because you took your time
Is that the word no is sometimes the right way to go

THE JOURNEY BEGINS

It's said that a journey begins one step a time
It also important to remember it starts in your mind
Although it may seem like your progress is so slow
If you stay consistent – you will see yourself grow!

THE POWER OF A SMILE

We all need to smile more because a smile is a powerful expression. It can make a mood changing statement. It can also show with little doubt how you feel. A smile can also be a request to change someone's emotional state at a certain time. Let your smile make its own positive statement!

YOUR SPOKEN WORDS

Be careful of just what you do and what you say
Your words can— carry a whole lot of weight
So always try to say things that lift and inspire
To help fill someone's soul with hope & desire

MAKE IT HAPPEN!

Too many of us live our lives
waiting for something to happen.
Have we forgotten we have the power
to make things happen?

WHEN YOU ARE WHO YOU ARE

You are so beautiful when you are who you are. Let me take that a step further and say the beauty I see in you is reflected outward because it is easy to accept you just as you are. So, we need to be honest with ourselves and be the person we were meant to be. Then beautiful we all will be.

Thought for the day #3

Unbelievable

Most things that seem unbelievable usually
are just that: Unbelievable!

DARK DAYS

Dark days help you to appreciate when the sun is shining. When will we again see the light? I want to see the light of a new and adventurous morning and a time to freely do almost anything that I desire to do. I would like to take a trip to the mall and enjoy a pretzel at a seating area. One day I want to venture outside and not be compelled to wear a surgical mask or even see others wearing them.

Oh, how I missed going to a matinee movie along with my own box of buttered popcorn. Can't I watch the news that does not speak first of the pandemic? I long for a time when I can again wallow in freedom! Being free comes in many different ways. In my heart I know there are days full of sunshine that are due to all of us. For me it cannot come quick enough!

SQUIRRELS IN THE ATTIC

How did they get in? I never hear gnashing or noise in the corner of the house! Yet they became a very unwelcomed guest. My journey to excavate them came next with a pretty penny paid. First came the exterminator who made a claim oh no they will never get thru the wire mesh that I am installing. I will give you a 60-day warranty. Seems like clockwork but as the warranty ended, so did the unwanted guest return! Through my frustration that company will never be used again, nor will I provide a referral!

Next to alleviate my guest I used as I will call them just company number two. Now the entry point was repaired, and the company said we will leave a trap in place for a couple of weeks and let us know if you hear anything and we will return. Occasionally, I heard scurrying across the ceiling and by now I am on fire with anger! For three weeks I could not even get a response from company number two.

Finally, after about a month, there was noise in the attic and the guest had found his destiny in the trap! Yours truly anxiously went into the attic to evict our guest. I waited for company number two to come and reclaim his trap and rid us of our unwanted visitor. I cannot start to tell you how much I spent to make it happen. I had to remove two large bushes at cost because that was one way for them to get to the roof top. So now there is peace and quiet in the attic.

I have no use for squirrels in any way shape or form. Any comment I have about squirrels will never be favorable and you will never hear me say they are cute. They are little living devils; with their minds set on destroy your attic and yard or surroundings. Enough said!

SUNSHINE

(sing song)

Sunshine, oh how I love the sunshine,

Sunshine, everybody loves the sunshine. Golden days, sunrays, and bright clear skies. I place the emphasis on warm weather and the fact that sunshine gives me a mental high.

Sunshine, golden rhymes I am on cloud nine nothing can make me feel better. I want to let it be known that you touch my soul. You are the one thing I give permission to start my day. As a matter of fact, I would not have it any other way!

When you peek through the sides of the blinds you also tell me that it is time to go! You tell me that those obstacles that stand in my way I cannot allow them to crush my day.

Sunshine, lifeline, by design oh how I wish I could have you with me every day. Sunshine you allow me to focus on each new adventure. I don my sunglasses and you ride with me as I travel across town. When I walk down the street, I feel your warm heat. Oh, sunshine please shine down on me!

(sing song)

Do what I do what I do when I do what I'm doing in the sunshine. My life, my life, my life, In the sunshine.

LAMENTS OF A FAN

We usually become a fan of a certain team by choice. Yet there are other reasons we become fans. Many become fans because they personally know a player or coach, they simply want to root for the home team or by family tradition. There is joy and pleasure being a fan of a winning team but what about if your loyalty is to a team that has not won for years? That is the sheer anguish, let me take a minute to write about it. The team you are a fan of has been bad for so long that you actually pray that in your lifetime you will see them win again. That has nothing to do with even winning a championship!

You don't get paid to be a fan, but you do pay to be a fan. I am speaking of buying tickets to games or even having season tickets. Attending almost any game on the professional level is awfully expensive. Yet there is an excitement to be a part of the actual event; even more so if you are supporting a team with a winning tradition. As evidence by this pandemic fans make the games more exciting! Their empty seats are replaced by cardboard figures which incidentally the fans pay for. As I stated earlier you pay to be a fan.

The other seats in the lower portions of the stadiums are covered with large business advertising their companies or logos. There is still money to be made even if the fans are not in the stadiums. When in the stadiums thousands of fans plan vacations around attending a game in the city of the team they support. Fans plan trips around attending games for their favorites. So, when this pandemic finally ends, I would love to see professional teams do even more to show their appreciation for their fans.

At this time for most professional teams, they will still continue to make millions of dollars because of the network contracts. Let us not forget that they also have a billion-dollar business in selling team clothing and paraphernalia. Remember fans it is a business and for us it depends on how much we are willing to spend to support a team when you can easily watch most games from home or listen on Sirius xm radio. I commend you all for being fans. I want to be honest I too struggle as a fan. I feel your pain, and I decided to limit my spending in supporting the teams I follow.

WHEN IT RAINS

From the coziness of my bed, I am awakened as the rain loudly pounds my windowsill. The rain plays its on song with its on special melody resounding from whatever it comes in contact with. The song it plays can be measured by the intensity and pace of the raindrops as they fall. We beg for rain when the earth around us is dry and barren. We tend to get upset when it rains for a prolonged amount of time. We all are on guard when we drive in a rainstorm and we look to gently navigate our cars to our destination.

There are many famous statements about the rain two of my favorites are: the calm before the storm and sunshine after the rain. Rain can be both good and bad at times, but we cannot underscore its importance in our lives. A gentle spring rain in the eyes of many is a beautiful thing. Prolonged rain can cause flooding and destruction and for that we all hold our breath. On the calmer side, I genuinely enjoy a quick rain shower.

I accept the blessing of rain when I do not have to water my garden or flowers. I take it a step further and make sure I have an empty bucket to receive the gift of rainwater from above. I will use it a few days later. In short, I love the rain! I love to be mentally rocked to sleep by the rain in the comfort and safety of my home.

PREACHING TO THE CHOIR

Just as frustrating as it is writing this piece. I feel frustration when I call most businesses for assistance. First it starts with "Due to the number of calls your wait time could be up to 30 mins". Try complaining to a large company about service and see if you get a call or response. Pretty much they disregard us contacting them and put us at the mercy of frustration even more. Never more has communication been needed by the consumer. We call and get voice prompts that tell us to tell them what we want.

When we try to explain they tell us how we should answer. That my friend is preaching to the choir. They only need the consumer for his business never again for his loyalty because the world is so full of followers, large business simply realizes that there will be someone else coming behind you. I don't have a solution to the preaching to the choir problem, but I try to keep my business in order, so I won't have to hear those hated words. You are in cue or your hold time is 20 minutes. Oh, how frustrating it is!

Thought for the day #4

Inspiration

Many times, one will have to reach deep inside themselves and find their own inspiration. It is not always good to wait for someone else to inspire you.

INSIDE THE SPIRAL NOTEBOOK

Though it has changed over the years, it still in essence is the same. It now may come in the form of a Microsoft word doc, a scan disc, a memory stick or even a backup memory data block. Some of its contents may first start out as a thought or an idea that's written on a napkin, a piece of paper, a brown bag or in in my case sometimes even in the palm of my own hand! Any poem, story or thought from the notebook can be lost or mistakenly removed. Once that happens your bad feelings are so hard to soothe. I hate to say it but the notebook itself can even be lost! Try carrying around a scan disc in your pocket and see what will eventually happen. If you lose it; I bet, you can never rewrite your favorites line for line. It's mostly because some of those pieces has not been performed in front of a waiting audience. The writer feels the lost material has so much potential.

The spiral notebook, I can't explain its importance. It shows your beginning, your growth, and your writing adjustments over the years. The spiral notebook develops recitals, memoirs, quotes and of most importance: books. These books will help writers to leave their marks whether big or small. So back it up please, back it up with extra copies, and an extra data disc. By any means possible. It's one of the most important things you could ever do as a writer. Hold on very tight to your spiral notebook.

HIDE ME FROM THE RAIN

Hide me from the rain not from rain drops
but from the things that bring us down
and when they come around

I can persevere because I don't feel bound
Hide me not from the downpour of a storm
but from situations that can cause me harm

Hide me from isolation and trepidation
from self-doubt and fear
and from the mindless thoughts and material things

that I once sought— keep me safe even from myself!
I seek safety from the enemy when he or she
may sit or stand right next to me!

Hide me from the disguises that we can wear
Especially when we put up a front
and give the impression that we care

The storms of life are not always water filled
where we can simply dry ourselves off
The circumstances can be deadly—

they come with a high cost!
So, for my hedge of protection
and for your trust and direction

I feel secure as I know you will
continue to hide me from the rain

A PIECE OF HEAVEN?

The gardener did everything including special care
to nourish the flowers he was always there
Nurturing, watering, weeding and cultivating
just like a baby the plants were there waiting

He prepares the soil, and protects them from insects
He gives them an environment to grow as he reflects
As they grow and mature their beauty we all see
because of his diligence they grow unintrusive and free

Just like the gardener, the church works for its congregation
remarkably similar; I am sure you observed the relation
A church is caring, loving and kind
bringing its people together and for growing it takes time

A church is a safe environment to grow and to praise
and when we are low our spirits will be raised
the preacher gives sermons like water that causes plants to grow
if we consistently worship our spirits will want more

So, they both are maybe a piece of heaven? Both provide guidance and caring, and they allow us to grow and to love just like our heavenly father from above.

I RECEIVE IT!

God's love is unconditional!

I consider all this and much more:

My life and my own song
A home I can call my own
A bed to retire to at night
Waking to a new day with a smile on my face
Coffee in the morning and a job to report to everyday
Transportation to take me along the way
Reasonable health and strength
Simple things like flowers and plants to beautify my home
my favorite vegetables I grew them on my own
I have food for strength and the ability to survive
and I offer thanks for each day I'm alive
for family and friends
and a big back yard
a gentle spring breeze
I offer prayers on my bended knees
for football and baseball and summer cookouts
Thanksgiving and Christmas
Celebrations I could not do without
for every time I travel and safely return
to be ever grateful of the things in life I've learned
In this state of the our world I can't take for granted
his grace, mercy and his unconditional love
I receive it!

HE SUSTAINS ME

During my darkest storm
My inner spirits are still warm
No matter how low I seem to go
I will not accept the word no
    (for he sustains me)

When I'm lost and confused
Or when I feel tired and not amused
When I've lost structure and direction
He's there to give me peace and protection
    (he sustains me)

And thru my greatest heartbreaks
When I prayed the Lord my soul to take
Yet I know I really want to live
To this ole world I have so much to give
    (he still sustains me!)

He even protects me from my own self
From foolish thoughts as if I didn't need help
You see I'm not a finish product (nope)
But you're looking at someone who has hope
    (because he truly sustains me)

When given a vision of a brand new dream
When others doubted me as bad as it seemed
He brought forth confidence and gave me a plan
That dream then came true as I took the stand
(so underserving but he still sustains me!)

You see I live every day for a chance at the prize
To have eternal life and it can't be disguised
Humbly I offer thanks with true appreciation
    For all you have done thru my many situations

READY FOR A CHANGE

Make America strong again; that is the slogan that Donald Trump promoted and sold to millions of his supporters. He even had t-shirts and hats bearing the slogan. Yet in his scandalous tour of office as president, did he make the U.S. stronger? America now is a place of tremendous divide! Donald Trump did much to contribute to that divide. So many secrets during his tour as president and situations that the office of president should have addressed yet he chose not to. In the end he lost his bid to serve a second term. In his disappointment, he voiced that the counts were off in certain states and that the election was taken from him. The way he presented it to his followers he made it seem like they lost the election as well.

The pro march to support Donald Trump will go down in infamy in American history. It will remain one of the darkest days ever. Hundreds of his supporters stormed the U. S. Capitol and received little resistance to enter the building. It indeed was a sad sight and a terrible way for a defeated president to finish his term. The thought here for me is people can be manipulated and changed to support a devil in disguise. Freedom of choice is a right in America but at the same time you have to do your homework. A president should be a leader, but he should be compassionate to all people. Extraordinarily little compassion was shown to Americans as we are in year two of this covid pandemic. The new president elect Biden may or may not be the answer and only time will tell. I do not think he could be much worse. America is so ready for a change!

I AM READY FOR CHANGE

Ready for change!
America should now be ready for change!
He said let's make America again strong but let me talk
about some of the things that went wrong.
His was a scandalous term and right now is America any stronger?
America now sits at the crossroad when it comes to social injustice.
Law enforcement can still pretty much murder people of color
and the judicial system will acquit.
It happens again and again
There is explosion coming!
And speaking of explosions!
in the end his bid for a second term ended under accusations
of voter counting irregularities.
Once he said it his followers believed him!
During a short speech in his Pro Trump rally: he said
"Let's make our way to the U. S. capitol."
Let us fight for our rights and he went out with a very loud
explosion! One of historic proportions an attempted takeover of
the U.S. capitol! When all of America needed you only tweeted
as COVID-19 raged on you stood unfazed.
You continued to speak and tweet on election fraud saying truly
little to encourage a hurting world let alone America.
In the end it was the voting count that did you in.
Now we do not know what the future holds but we have hope.
The classic song states "Everything must change nothing stays
the same". In this case thank God! Let us go out with old and try
something new. I am so ready for change!

MUSIC: THE QUEEN OF MY SOUL

Growing up as a babe, I was spoon-fed music. It was music of many styles and genres; gospel, quartet, soul, blues, and traditional jazz; they all crowded my young ears. So much that even today music is part of my lifeblood. Today I honor my love for Music with an acrostic poem set to the letters that comprise that incredibly special word.

M   represents the Melody that catches my ear

U   <u>Unique</u> sounds that I love and hold dear

S   Is for <u>Songs</u> the countless thousands that make up my collection

I   Is for <u>Inside</u> the music, Inside the beat I find myself

C   represents <u>Constant</u> my search for good music never ends

Music you are the Queen of my Soul.

Thought for the day #5

It's never too late

Its never too late to try something new, a new hobby, take a class or learn a new dance but first you have to be willing to take a chance.

ALL ABOARD! RIDING WITH HARRIET TUBMAN

I don't confess to have the time to tell her whole story. I just wanted to take a moment and give her a bit of glory for doing her job so well. It truly touches my heart and I hope you can tell. She was fearless, creative, and patient. She was smarter than given credit for because she learned how to think quick. She was a leader and a disciplinarian who on the move even learned some very witty tricks . Her story still should inspire those of us who think we have no way out. If we look deep within ourselves, you will see we have plenty of clout. Today we all ride on a different type of rail system that is just as oppressive and corrupt as the body of the government that allowed slavery to exist in the first place.

ALL ABOARD! ALL ABOARD! DESTINATION: FREEDOM!

This conductor would proudly state she never lost a passenger. So many trips and never a slip! Over 300 souls were freed maybe even some distant relatives of you and me. She was born a slave who was destined to lead the way. Dangerous as her job was, she was up to the task. To help those oppressed remove the mask (of slavery that is) Because she feared that she may be sold, she up and ran away to freedom. Traveling by night and in day remaining out of sight she continued her plight until she arrives in Philadelphia, Pa. a free woman! Working and saving her money she would return to free her family and others who were bold enough to endure the physical trip with her. Thus, was born the Underground Railroad.

If you think she wasn't smart, then let me tell you how she made it work. She stirred clear of where she knew danger lurked. Then with a bit of chance but never out in the open would she prance. By travelling on Saturday night, she could make those necessary flights by having two free days until runaway notices were placed in newspapers on Monday. If a fugitive baby cried, she would give them a sedative type of drug to help them sleep as they went bye, bye. Harriet even carried a gun and would threaten to use it if fugitives got tired or wanted to return. She would not allow her other passengers to be burned. They were freedom bound. There would be no turning around!

She became highly sought and with a lofty price she was worth— $40,000 dollars. Dead or alive but don't count on it! She knew how to survive! She was even sometimes called Moses because she was leading her people to the Promised Land and for freedom she took the ultimate stand! She was highly respected by black leaders such as Frederick Douglass and John Brown. Harriet would still live an incredibly long life. She died in Auburn, New York in 1913.

WE LIVED WITH A LEGEND
MAYA ANGELOU

Many stories have been told; many poems have been written as well. We still continue to look back and say that God was really, really good to her and she was indeed a great role model. A role model not just for black women but black men as well. As a matter of fact, she was a role model for all people. She was a lady of charm and a woman of great verse; I am eternally saddened that I never had a chance to hear her speak or perform live. That would have been a memory that I would cherish for the rest of my life.

Your legend will grow even greater in your death. Legends never really die in the eyes and hearts of those who sincerely love them. Every one of us knows from the first note the sound of Marvin Gaye's voice. We have embedded in our hearts the great roar and the smoothness of Luther Vandross' one of a kind voice.

For those of us who loved and adored her she will forever be with us. A new wave of poets will embrace her writing style. Maya's work will continue to mentor us just as she did while the legend lived amongst us. The greatest tribute that I gave and could still give her comes from a piece that I wrote entitled "If I could". The poem asks a question what you would do if you have an opportunity to talk with a great black American hero or legend. I say again: If I could I I would close my eyes and listen intently to Maya Angelou as she recites just for me: her moving poem "I know why the caged bird sings". What an honor that would be.

INTRODUCTION: THE BLACK SOLDIER

Take a moment to reflect on the black soldier; he was then and is today a warrior. He is a fighting machine who has natural instincts for survival. The black soldier helped change the outcome of the American civil war. They open the safe expansion into the west as the vaunted Buffalo soldiers. They fought gallantly in World War 1 and received little or no honor! These same men could not board American naval ships to return home from war! In spite of that injustice, they served gallantly during World War II. There they wore the names of the Red Ball Express, the Tuskegee airmen, the Black panthers, 761st armored tank division and still the 9th & 10th cavalry and the 24th infantry Buffalo Soldiers divisions. Through the Korean war, the mindless and endless Viet nam war, Iran, Iraq and in Afghanistan the black soldier has been a model of unheralded consistency. Although all servicemen and women alike should be honored and appreciated, this is special just for current and retired black soldiers male and female alike. I thank you for your bravery and for your endless sacrifices.

A TRIBUTE TO THE BLACK SOLDIER

Through Americas conflicts always right there
Though scorned by many yet showing they cared
They created a rich history that we must preserve
Injustices they dealt with— at times thrown a curve

These truly are the proud
Men who fought with pounding hearts
Performing missions under a cloud
Scorned & doubted from the very start

In war— receiving no honor what comes next?
A world's journey that ends unrecognized
Returning with issues in full effect
Forever in my prayers yet always scrutinized

Black heroes that history many times will hide
These truly are our heroes
Ingrained— their memories of wars remain
Sometimes creating a tolerance of zero
They deserve respect that's their refrain

For body parts and missing limbs
For A tour of duty thousands of miles away
They deserve hope, not a return to the dark & dim
I know these words will not make it okay
I give respect, admiration and thanks on this day

THEY WERE BUFFALO SOLDIERS

Courage and patriotism are not restricted to a single group of people or culture. Yes, that is true— but we black Americans, young and especially those older know of the fighting spirit of the black soldier. As far back as the civil war, many times their acts of heroism were underplayed or simply ignored. Today I direct my writing to my favorite military hero: the "Buffalo Soldier." Their regiments (9th and 10th Cavalry, 24th and 25th Infantry) are prolific in American military history.

The black soldier was first given inferior equipment and training and many volunteers did not receive uniforms and boots upon enlistment. In spite of that they still wanted to be soldiers! In your spare time please watch the true accounts of the movie: "Glory." As segregated units the black soldier actually helped turn the civil war in the favor of the union.

These regiments helped blaze the western frontier. The American Indians were the first to call them Buffalo soldiers because of their dark skin color and the coarseness of their hair. These soldiers possessed the same toughness of the buffalo— thus the name: Buffalo soldier! I am proud to say they aided tremendously in the development of the United States as a world power. The courage of these Black soldiers meant not only valor in the face of danger, but a spirit to serve to their country despite discrimination, segregation, and repressive laws.

From inception in 1866 until integration after 1948, the Buffalo Soldier regiments were segregated, and with only a few exceptions, the officers in charge were Caucasian. Nevertheless, soldiers of the four Black regiments overcame extreme adversity on the battlefield and at home to establish themselves as among the most effective military units in the Army. After desegregation, in the military, the 9th and the 10th cavalry units are still active in the U. S. army today! *Ready and Forward* was the motto adopted by the 10th Cavalry.

READY & FORWARD THE MOTTO OF THE 10TH CAVALRY

Ready & forward!
Courageous and brave
Once captive and enslaved
Fighting though segregated
In conditions so degrading

Ready & forward!
Fighting adversity
With a sense of urgency
Black units supreme
Once oppressed & now mean

Ready & forward!
The 9th & 10th cavalry
Western America they freed
From 1866 to 1944
Great black American lore

Ready & forward!
A motto of great pride
My respect I won't hide
The 9th and 10th Calvary
A stirring part of black history

Thought for today #6

Tomorrow is the best ending to yesterday.
We are given one more chance at life.

OH WHAT A DAY!

There is the blessed day of Sunday and all the days of the entire week. There are dark days and sad days, but we still have to continue on our way. We enjoy Holidays, pay days, workdays off days and the list goes on and on. But there is something incredibly special about birthdays because without them there is no you or no me.

So may today bring you first happiness, the feelings of giving love and being loved by those closest to you. May you continue to enjoy health and strength and continue to be someone who encourages not only their family, but co workers and in general those that are in your circle of friends and acquaintances. On this your special day enjoy it like never before!

Happy Birthday

OUT OF THE DARKNESS

All around us there is darkness. There is an image of pitch black and a thought of no direction and no movement. The world somehow seemed at a complete standstill. So how long can this go on? Through the despair there shone just a tiny flicker of light. A vision of sight which provides for the world a beacon of hope and purpose.

In these hard times only the strong survive! The media will try to tell us how to cope but it is prayers and belief in the father who will give us hope. The hope we see when we look for even a tiny light at the darkest point of our troubles. One might call it the light at the end of the tunnel.

In a world now so full of isolation, corruption, destruction, social inequities, man-made pandemics, selfish leadership, and the whole world seems to just to hold on. Hope is the rope that we all need to hold so very tight. We look forward to a new day with a new resolve and more caring for the family and friendships that we sometimes have taken for granted. Out of the darkness there is hope.

Thought for the day #7

Children are our future give them the
knowledge of your lifetime.

SAVE THE CHILDREN

Life's most precious commodity are our children. So, are we doing all we can to save the children? Let's save them from hurt, harm and danger. Let's not allow them to fall into the hands of some stranger! Along with affection we must provide for them protection and a safe home. We must give them stability in their surroundings which promote serenity and a sense of calm. The world is ready to snatch them; use them and abuse them leaving them with a neglected and insecure state of mind. Save the children is my passionate and heartfelt plea. Save and protect the children! It starts with you and me!

HOW DEEP IS MY LOVE

The depth of my love runs deep. It's a love that stands the test of time. It's a love that's full of appreciation and during times of turbulence its steadfast and unmovable. My love is a model of longevity. You can count on me. My love offers protection, affection and security all rolled into one.

You must believe I am not afraid to show it! It's yours to keep through hard times and good times; whether with smiles or frowns, my love will always be sound. Just like the measured depths of the world's deepest river the congo-Lualaba; I give the full measure of love that I have just to you.

I promise it will one day grow to match the depth of that mighty river! So how deep is my love: It's river deep! It's mountain high!

24-7 AND 365 A LOVE THAT WON'T GO AWAY

Wouldn't it be nice if one could find a love that would last for a lifetime; 24-7 and 365 days a year? It would be an old-fashioned love that makes you feel so alive. It would be a love that is based on togetherness, not monetary gains, not fantastic looks or world or social status.

Most of us want to be loved for who we really are. Inside that love you feel complete because it makes you feel whole, deep down into the pit of your soul. People change and over a period of time no one stays the same. It almost makes it impossible to find that kind of blessing.

In a not so perfect world, we should not have to look for perfection. We should want to be treated with love and respect and if it last and sustains then we still may wind up getting our 24-7 and 365 forever and a day.

INSURGENCY IN AMERICA

Insurgency in America no that can't be!

This is supposed to be a democracy. The land of the brave and the home of the free! Where peaceful protests for Black Lives Matter were controlled by presidential ordered National Guardsmen. Yet hundreds of Trump supporters were able to storm the U. S. Capitol which was under protected and yet they knew it could be trouble due to the amount of people at the Pro-Trump rally. Insurgency in America are you kidding me?

Hatred and destruction all in plain sight and don't you dare call it Patriotism because it is not. I am left with so many feelings of distrust. If it were black and brown people how many would have died? It would have been shoot first and ask questions much later. It has left a lifetime scare on American democracy. Insurgency in America live for the entire world to see!

Destroy, hurt, harm, and even kill and on his way out this appeared to be Donald Trumps' greatest thrill. It leaves America with a bad taste. What is this country's fate? Right now, there is a double standard in America. We can only hope for a brighter day with justice for all people. Crimes of this magnitude should not go unpunished. Racism and race superiority must be brought under control. It is supposed to be one country with justice for all.

THE COST OF A SMILE

How much would you charge for a smile? Would it cost the same price as a laugh? Would a big smile cost more than a quick grin? Would you prefer a robust laugh over a light chuckle? Would it bother you if someone just rolled in the floor with laughter? Or is it ok to just acknowledge that funny joke with light movement or no movement at all? Do you temper your laugh, or do you just let go? When you watch a funny movie or sitcom can you relax enough to really enjoy it or does your subconscious say this is not really fun or even stupid?

In this world there are so many problems, so many issues we need smiles, and we need laughter! We only need to look at our own shortcomings and issues and see that we all need to learn how to laugh and smile more. It won't change or correct our life issues but at least it gives us a moment or two of enjoyment or release. I think we all need that. The next time someone says something that is really funny just let yourself go for a moment. The true cost of a smile or a laugh is just learning how to release that emotion.

This poem was birthed through my love for Ecclesiastes 3 To everything there is a season.

LET YOUR VOICE BE HEARD

Many times we are just silent partners
maybe not wanting to get involved
Many times we are just onlookers
we think that we can't make a difference
even more so today don't let your time
to speak pass in silence!

In certain situations, it will cause you regrets
so fight those types of battles with your voice
say what you have to say be direct and to the point
because if you don't those empty thoughts
will forever haunt

There comes a time to speak out
not a time to harbor silence
a time to stand your ground
a time to make sure your voice is heard
you will be glad that you did!

You don't have to be overly loud
yet you must be assertive and confident
knowledgeable and well versed in your
comments

Friends, family, and constituents
will notice the difference
and with this change will come respect
people around you will listen when you speak
You indeed have something to say!

GOLD

We search our entire lives for material wealth and material things. Sometimes we already have it. Yet we do not realize it. Sometimes it is right there in front of us in the form of a person we love very much. So, I am saying you are my gold! Am I concerned with how many karats or weight? No, you are precious but not a possession. You are a blessing. Like a fine wine highly priced but aging so genuinely nice. You are like an expensive cologne the aroma is enticing and inviting. When you enter you light up the room with your presence. Gold shines brightly and is evident for all to see. You radiate just by being who you are.

ALONE

It's not always in the presence of being by yourself,
one can feel alone even within a crowd
or a sporting event where its vocal and loud
or in your automobile in traffic with so many others around
kind of like being the only penny in a pocket full of change
All alone!

You can feel alone waiting in a concession line with strangers
or as you walk quickly to your car to get out of danger
Alone is a state of mind that many of us can't handle
likening it to being a small picture on an oversized mantle.

Don't let the state of being alone work against you
when you feel that way here is what you should do
Work very hard to become your own best friend
trust your own heart until the very end

Choose to be alone at times by your own choice
you don't always have to speak to hear your own voice!
Don't let world isolation and travel restraints

make you feel locked in as a prisoner
Alone is a state of mind that with a plan of action almost anyone
can control those moments of being alone.

I LOOK TO THE HILLS
PSALM 121

When I look to the hills
I began to feel my relief
It brings a sense of calm
Into my spirit it runs deep

When I look to the hills
I give to the father my problems
His loving presence is here
He'll show me how to solve them

When I look to the hills
I'm not shaken, I'm strong
for there I find peace
I forsake those sad moans

For I belong to the keeper
and quickly I discovered
No matter how much despair
I have the ability to recover

Under any strenuous situation
Thru adversity, I must stand tall
I am assured he protects me
He will not allow me to fall

He always keeps his eye on me
I am always within his sight
My foot is planted firmly
knowing that I rest well at night

I have safety both day and night
Because I have looked to the hills
He is the shade at my right hand
I'll overcome because of his will

Look always to the hills for the answer
No reason to become withdrawn
Roadblocks will always abound
with our father, we are never alone!

THIS IS NOT AMERICA

This is not the America we once knew. I wonder where could it be? They say we're still living in the land of the free. This can't be America how could things so quickly change? Where did the idiom of time go where we all looked so much to our golden past? Our country is in such need of leadership and there is so much to be corrected. During the last four years nearly, everyone has been affected. Millions chose to follow the Trump leadership and now our country has lost faith and we desperately need it.

A worldwide pandemic, home grown terrorists in action right in plain sight. Presidential leadership helping to stoke the fires. Just as a weed can grow almost anywhere; believe that America can grow terrorist too! History says come to America where your dreams can grow, under the circumstance I just don't know. There is so much work for us to do as a nation. We fight social injustices, thousands of job loss, governmental protocol and tax changes that enhance large businesses.

The rich become wealthier—the middle class lose—and the poor as it seems will never rise. This is not America, but tell me what is it?

FINDING PEACE THROUGH THE STORM

In time life's storms will appear
we are so happy when they finally go
with them comes much fear
and things of which we just don't know

Relationships that were once calm
now they become visibly amiss
now there's an emotional balm
and words are spoken with risk

life gives constant reminders
of how hard we all must work
to treat each other more kind
prepare for the storms that lurk

you must take it to God in prayer
I guarantee you'll get much stronger
there is no reason to say life's not fair
you'll be able to endure much longer

when the storms of life finally clears
there will be yet another one coming
It brings no signs that you or I can hear
Life's storms doesn't give us a clear warning

SPEAKING HIS OWN THOUGHTS

Let me tell you about the Reverend Doctor Vernon Johns— a man who spoke his own mind. Though often brash and sometimes derogatory, he was one of the first black men who advocated equality for black and brown people. His views were not always accepted by even the churches or members that he pastored. This outspoken approach caused him to move from church to church. Yet in his own way he wanted blacks to speak up about what was going on around and against them. It was in essence the early moniker for todays' Black Lives Matter. How odd was it for a black man to be outspoken about police brutality and social injustices during those segregated years when white America could do pretty much whatever they wanted to black people and get away with it. Even today treatment of black and brown people have not really changed that much. They are just handled in different ways because the judicial system usually will find white cops not guilty. So, by these views the Black Lives Matter movement is not new. It finally has a title. The moral to this short story is maybe without the outspoken words of Dr. Vernon Johns there maybe would not have been the growth and acceptance of Martin Luther King as the civil rights movement was born and became a force for change. The fight for equality must continue and people have to be held accountable for unlawful actions against those people that they were sworn to protect. Though he gets extraordinarily little credit for his leadership and words for a call to action, his voice was needed. His voice was necessary. His determination and leadership must not be forgotten.

IF I COULD (A TRIBUTE TO WOMEN OF COLOR)

So many women of all denominations have made great contributions in society. So, I asked myself a question— what would I say to some incredibly special women of color whom I have great admiration for? Here is what I would say If I had that chance.

If I could chat with Mya Angelou; I would ask her to sign my copy of her book of poetry— Maya Angelou the complete book of poetry. I would ask her to recite for me lines from her famous poem: Caged Bird. The Caged bird sings of freedom!

If I could I would request a special mini concert from still one of my favorite singers Stefanie Mills. In the silhouette of a dimly lit stage, I would selfishly have her sing for me "Feel the fire". I would love that!

If I could speak with Mary Mcleod Bethune, I would ask her a million and one questions about how her dream of a school for young girls became Bethune Cookman university.

If I could I'd sit proudly beside Rosa Parks on that famous day when she said no! I will not go. I will not move! I would ride the freedom train with Harriet Tubman and sing for her "Wade in the water".

If I could I'd offer congratulations to Midshipman Sydney Barber, the U.S. Naval Academy's first black brigade commander. Then I would tell her how proud I am of her and how she is inspiring thousands of people to live their dreams and dream big.

If I could I would speak with Rosalind "Roz" Brewer who recently assumed her new role as CEO of Walgreens. I would ask her about her motivation and who inspired her as she climbed the ladder to success. She is the only Black woman currently serving as the head of a Fortune 500 company and just the third in history to achieve that milestone.

Finally and the most important today:

If could I would thank Dr. Kuzzmekia Corbett for her skill and expertise as the lead scientist on the Moderna Covid-19 Vaccine team. She still is maybe America's best kept secret, but she and her team have and will continue to save millions of lives through the deployment of the vaccine.

So, as we celebrate women's history month; women all over the world should be appreciated for your endurance, for all your sacrifices, for your burning desire to achieve and make your own statement, and finally for the many gains you have made to make this world a better place.

INHALE EXHALE JUST BREATHE

Just as during an examination: inhale exhale and breathe. This time it is to relive tension. The world we live in is full of frustrations with stress covering as if it's the topping on a cake. From day to day we wonder what will come next.

Inhale exhale and breathe. I don't have to tell you that stress kills, it causes feelings of depression and helplessness. In our lifetime everyone will experience it.

Inhale exhale and breathe, we see social injustices all over the world, our police state with racial profiling and brutality still ongoing. Corruptions with city and government officials, misuse of monies including Black Lives Matter contributions; the list is ongoing. Domestic violence is at an all-time high.

It seems every week there is a mass shooting— hold your breathe when you venture out. Just who can we really trust? I think we all better inhale then exhale and breathe. I am not asking you to accept social injustices, or some of the many crazy things going on in our world. I'm just asking you to look out for your own health so we can collectively band together and continue our fight for justice. Take moments to learn how to view your own life on the lighter side. Do some things that make you laugh and smile.

Our world is so full of corruption, consumption, collusion, and intrusion. The many good things that people do many times are never reported. These stories go untold and never get to calm our souls.

One last time and this is not yoga 101 or a breathing exercise it's a mental exercise. Inhale – exhale and just breathe. Imagine your mind free without any enemies. Imagine your life with little or no stress and feeling like you are truly blessed. This is what we all want! This is what we deserve! No matter what you are going through: take care of your mind and your body first.

LOOK ON THE BRIGHT SIDE

The songwriter sang:
Times may be rough, life may be tough but you must keep going
We feeling the pain we keep holding strain but we must keep fighting

Regardless of how it comes, we just can't surrender
We got to keep working towards a better future
Look on the bright side, look on the bright side for the bright side is where were going!

Let us not forget we are the fortune— some of the people who are still around. We have been able to stay out of harm's way or even recover from the dreaded and hated virus covid-19. The picture now is more clear but still there remains fear. Wear your mask, wash your hands again and again. Maintain your six-foot distance even though some are not adhering. Don't take unnecessary chances! These are small measures to ask for survival.

Look on the bright side, That's where we're going.

Loved one's and friends have been lost, the world has paid a great cost. Jobs are forgone, marriages abandoned and some of our children are out of control. The negatives of the pandemic touches deep inside our souls.

Yet I look to the bright side because that's where I am going.

I'm prayerful and thankful for everyday and even for being idle sometimes because I am still here! Because I have persevered; I have new hobbies, I have better designs on my life and my health. I dance, I run, I walk and I teach aerobics with zeal like never before. I cherish the friendships and the few close relatives that give purpose to my life. I live life hard everyday and do everything to fulfill my life. During these stressful times, I want you to do the same. Please do everything that you can to make yourself happy!

Look to the brighter side, look to the brighter side because the bright side is where we're going!

ACCOUNTABILITY

I ushered my friend off the phone so I could watch the verdict of the George Floyd murder trial. I sit there glued to the screen in anticipation but also with large amounts fear and trepidation. As the judge read the verdict and on count one of guilty, a small tear formed in the corner of my eye. He then read verdict two and it too was guilty! Finally count number three was read and it was also guilty! Now tears were in both eyes and for the moment I felt a sigh of relief.

Relief that there would not be more violence and destruction because the judicial system found the accused Darren Chauvin not guilty. It's a victory for justice but it is not a moment to relax because there is so much more work to be done. Change is not over night especially when racism and bias is so deeply rooted as it is in America. Thousand of black men and women and people of color have been killed since America first brought slaves to what is now called the United States. As we celebrate this victory lets not forget about Brianna Taylor, Michael Brown, Freddie Gray and Donte Wright among many others who were killed by Police who never were held accountable. Its time for us to no longer be the Strange Fruit that is hanging from a tree. Justice means changing the policing system and holding bad and biased policemen and women accountable, Victory is not ours but the battle rages on for justice. Black Lives do matter.

Thought for today #8

Worrying is like carrying a 50 lb. backpack once you put it down you feel so much better!

DON'T WORRY BE HAPPY

Needless to say, this poem was written especially for me. It was written for the many times I worried about things that were out of my control. I worried because I felt isolated, and I worried because of how I thought others perceived me. Now I just try to be the best version of myself and accept the person that I have become. I am my own best friend.

How significant is it to worry? When we do, we usually focus on allowing something that's negative to weigh heavily on our mind. Worrying will cause us some trying times. Has worrying ever paid a mortgage, landed anyone a job, paid a bill or tuition, dinner or a special event? I don't think so! The challenge is to learn what God has provided to help us deal with things that happen to us in this broken world. Bad things happen and they sometimes happen to good people. It can quickly turn a smile to a frown. It can turn your sunshine into a dark cloud.

Worrying can defeat us when it replaces wise action with fearful emotion. To react with fear will detract from the present while doing nothing to prepare for the future; let alone tomorrow. Keep in mind there is a future beyond that misfortune we just went through. God wants us to read, pray, trust and obey; not necessarily in that order but just as long as we do it.

Read the bible again and again.

Pray unceasingly and that means we can pray anywhere and anytime.

Trust God in all that you do and in the things we cannot control.

Obey God! He wants us to be obedient— we know the difference between right and wrong! We must take action; we can't sit around and feel sorry for ourselves.

When we do we will know that trouble won't last always. When we believe in God we are no longer bound!

So don't worry be happy!

SOUL SEARCHING

We constantly search for almost everything.
Let me name just a few:
We search for better jobs
Shiny new cars
relationships to grow and hopefully last
we search for ways to hide issues that we know we have
for new products to improve our health
then we search for ways to grow and supplement our wealth
We even search for new tv shows to occupy our time
or a new gym or recreation center to help strengthen our body and mind.
I find that the search never ends!
Can I ask a question?
How many times do we search our own souls?
Can we look inside ourselves for a better view?
Can we see and do we like or even love the person we have become?
How can each of us become better with caring for the things that are important to us
We weren't created to achieve perfection, but we can ask God to reveal to us the things that we do not see even when our eyes are open wide! This will help us all to prepare for the missions of our lives and each of us have our own mission as it is very evident in this passage of scripture.
Hebrews 12:1 Since we are surrounded by such a great cloud of witnesses, let us throw off everything that hinders and the sin that so easily entangles. Let us run with perseverance the race marked out for us.

REFLECTIONS

Reflect if you will back to a good time that you once had. Think about the joy, the laughter and the experienced itself. How did it make you feel inside? For the past year many of us have very few things to reflect on. Yes, we are grateful to be alive; and sorrowful for family and friends who have lost their lives and or livelihood through this pandemic. So search if you may to any event that made you forget the current situation of the world and it just made you laugh or feel good if even for a few moments. Make sure you enjoy them mentally over and over again. Reflections take us back, but they also make us look forward to tomorrow and the good things hopefully they will bring.

EPILOG

Tomorrow could be a lifetime away. All we have is right now today. Please don't take for granted your tomorrows. Until I see you again, I want only the best for you. Thank you for enjoying my book.

J. L.

www.ingramcontent.com/pod-product-compliance
Lightning Source LLC
LaVergne TN
LVHW091604060526
838200LV00036B/985